BRENT'S WORLD

BARB SMITH

Outskirts Press, Inc.
Denver, Colorado

DEDICATION

I dedicate this book to my loving husband, Tim. Without his love and support, this book would not have been possible.

Tim, I love you more as each day passes.

These memories are not told in chronological order, but more as a collection of thoughts based on themes, and they are told as they came to me.

TABLE OF CONTENTS

CHAPTER 1
OPENING

Mary Lou and Herb were married February 8, 1958. They have three children. Their firstborn is Lynn, then Barbara, with Mickey arriving 15 months later. My mother's sister, Joanne, and her husband, Alton, are a big part of our lives. We are a close-knit family. We live within 20 miles of each other in Southeastern, Michigan. We get together often and are always together on holidays.

Brent Anthony was born August 5, 1982 to Barbara, his 19-year-old mother.

He was an unplanned pregnancy but a welcome delight when he arrived. He weighed in at 8 lbs 8 ozs, and was 21½ inches long. He was perfect in every way. Thankfully, Barb, as she liked to be called, had the support of her family. Her sister, Lynn, was her labor coach. She went with Barb to Lamaze classes, and participated in the birth every step of the way.

Brent's first year of life was spent living with his mother at her parents' home. A bond was formed with his grandparents during that first year that would carry on throughout Brent's entire life. His grandparents meant the world to him, and they felt the same way about him.

Brent and his Grandma, Mary Lou, had a lot in common. They were both full of energy, smart, and loved computers. They would spend hours together on her computers.

Brent had his Grandpa Herb's work ethic. They were both very hard workers. During his teenage years, Brent worked on a farm four summers in a row. The owner of the farm said that Brent was the hardest-working teen he had ever employed.

Brent made us all proud. He was a unique individual with a passion for living life to the fullest.

Brent passed away December 4, 2005 from the consequences of his drug and alcohol addiction.

Our family has been devastated by his death. There is a huge hole in all of our hearts.

As his mother, I'm compelled to share the story of his life and struggles. I also wanted to share of the love our family has for one another, and the love that Our Mighty God has shown us during this time. If it had not been for God's love and guidance, I do not believe any of us would have survived.

CHAPTER 2
CHILDHOOD

Brent was a very active child, he was always on the go. When he was three years old, I moved into a rental house in downtown Ypsilanti.

There were train tracks in front of the house. When we first moved in, every time the train went by, Brent would run to the front door and watch it. After about a week or so, he lost interest in that. Thankfully, the house had a fence in the front yard so I didn't have to worry about Brent getting hurt by the train.

Brent was up at the crack of dawn every morning. I worked afternoons, and when I got home from work, I couldn't fall asleep right away. I would watch all the late night talk shows. Brent would get up around 6:00am. He would run into my room and wake me up. I would fix him breakfast and then he would watch cartoons. I was very thankful that he was a TV watcher, because I could get another hour of sleep while he was interested in his shows. I would lie on one side of the couch, and Brent would lie on the other side. I would keep my feet on him and if he got up, it would wake me up.

Every day we went for walks. When the weather was nice, Brent would ride his big wheel. For those of you that have never heard of a big wheel, it looks like it sounds. The front wheel is big with a seat, with two small wheels in the back. Brent could ride like there was no tomorrow. When he was six years old, I entered him into a bike race at the Washtenaw County Police Station. He had a wonderful time racing the other kids. My mom also went with us to the race. We were so proud of him!

There was a school down the street from where we lived that had a playground.

Brent loved for me to push him on the swings.

He also loved to go down the slide. It didn't matter how high the slide was; he wasn't scared. I was always afraid he would fall off, but he didn't!

On Sunday afternoons, we would go to my mom and dad's house. Usually, my Uncle Alton and Aunt Joanne were there. Brent would get under the kitchen table and untie Uncle Alton's tennis shoes. Not sure what the fascination was with those shoes.

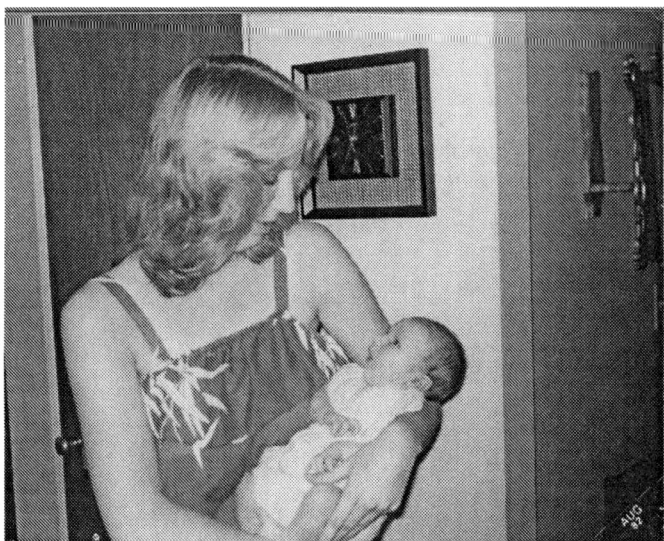

Mom and Brent at 1 week old

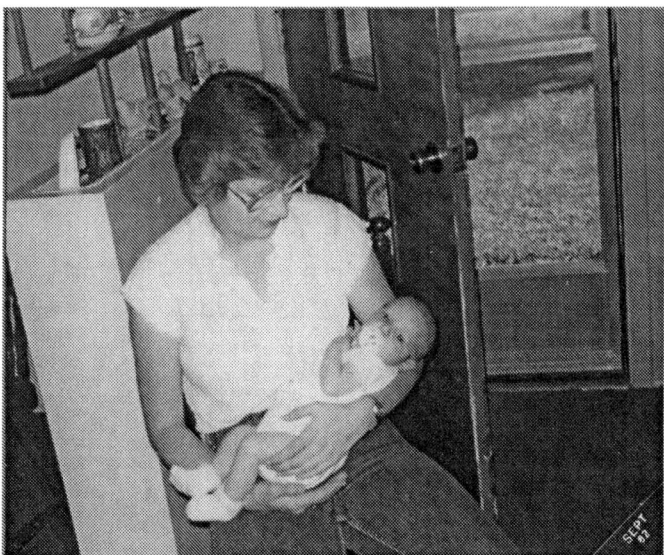

Aunt Lynn and Brent at 1 month old

Mom reading to Brent

Uncle Mickey's High School Graduation Day!

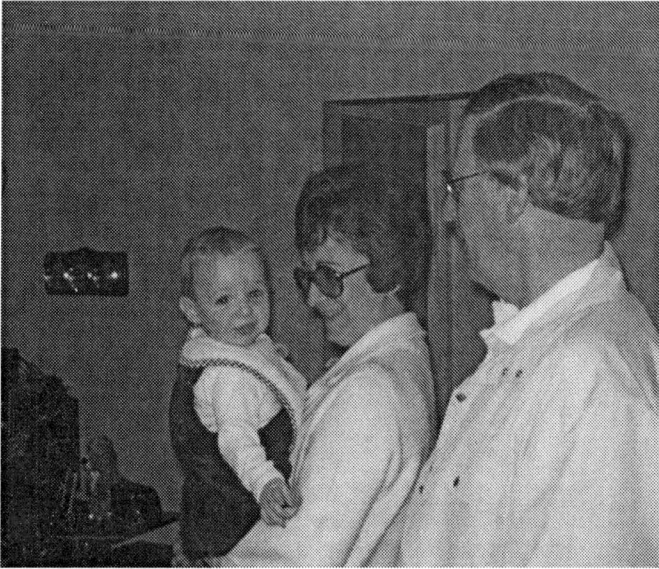
Uncle Alton and Aunt Joanne talking to Brent

Brent at 1 ½ years old

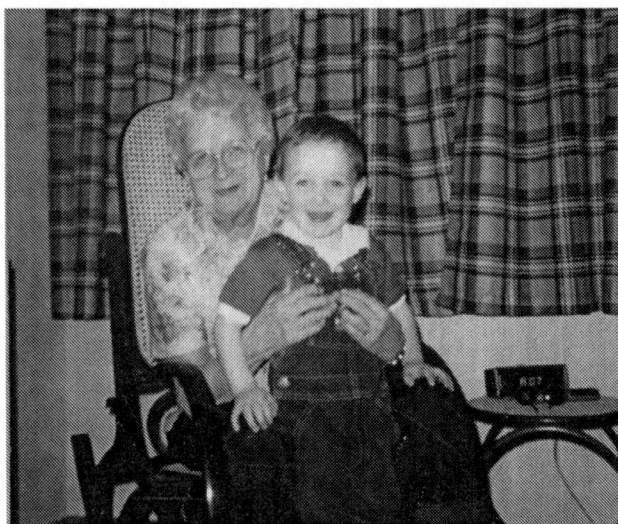
Brent was the apple of Great-Grandma Lucille's eye

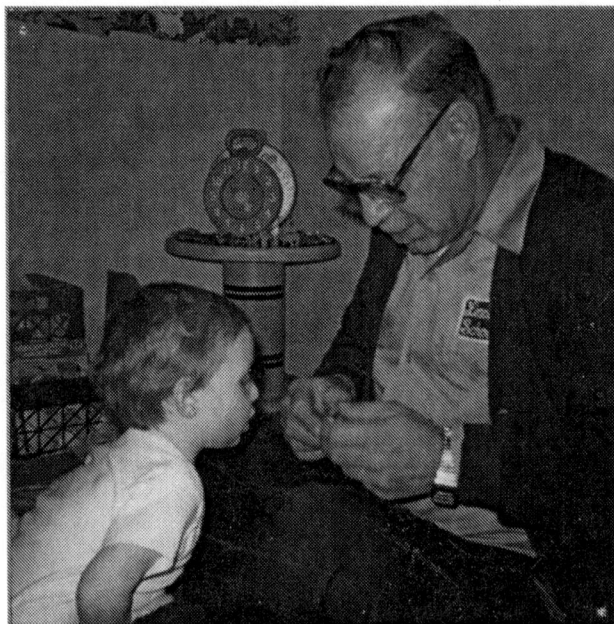
Grandpa Herb fixing one of Brent's toys

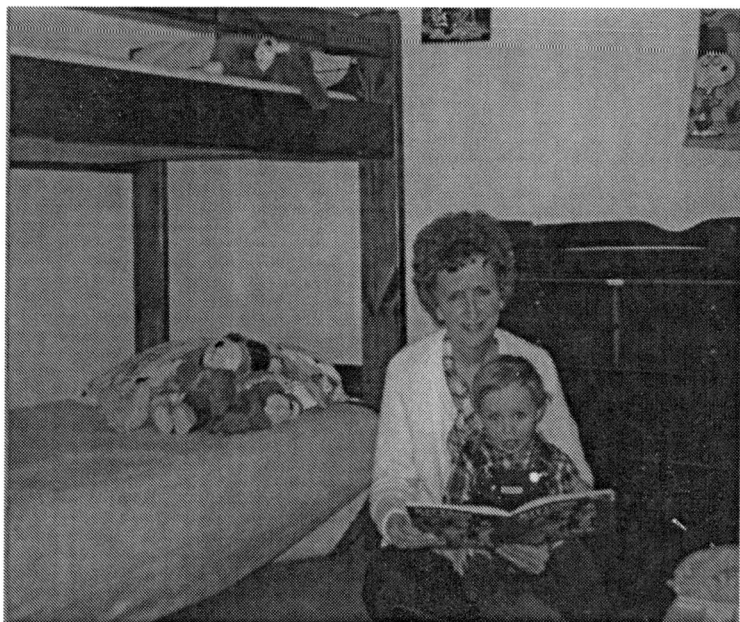
Grandma Mary Lou reading to Brent

Grandma Patty helping Brent color

CHAPTER 3
GRACE

When Brent was four years old, I married Jason. We wanted to add to our family as soon as we could. On April 27, 1987 I gave birth to a beautiful baby girl named Grace. Up until this time, Brent had my undivided attention. I tried to prepare him for her arrival. We talked about the baby coming and how he was going to be a good big brother.

I attended Lamaze classes, and they said to help the siblings feel a part of the birth, have them pick out a stuffed animal or small toy to put in the bassinet at the hospital. That way, when they came to visit, they would see the toy and feel a part of the event. Brent decided he would give Grace a small stuffed bunny. I made a big deal about how he was going to be such a wonderful big brother. When he got to the hospital, he was overwhelmed. It was hard for him to be away from me so he was not very excited about Grace. When it was time for him to leave, he was walking down the hallway and he started to cry.

Jason asked, "What's wrong?"

Brent said, "I want my bunny back!"

They went to the nursery and asked the nurse if Brent could have his bunny and she said, "Sure." I thought that was so cute!

When I got home from the hospital, Brent was a big help.

He would get diapers or anything I needed, I didn't have to move an inch! Any new mother would appreciate that!

About a week later, I took Brent for some one-on-one time to the local donut shop.

On the way there he said, "You know, Mom, I think we should go back to just me and you."

I said, "But what about Grace?"

He said, "Jason can keep her."

I said, "Wouldn't you miss her?"

He said, "No, we can visit."

I chuckled to myself about his suggestion.

He loved his new sister, but realized that she got a lot of my attention.

When Grace got a little older, I would lie her on a blanket with Brent in front of the TV. She would just stare at her big brother. He would rub her head during commercials!

They loved each other very much.

Brent, Aunt Trudy and Grace at a family gathering

Brent showing off his musical talents!

Brent and Grace

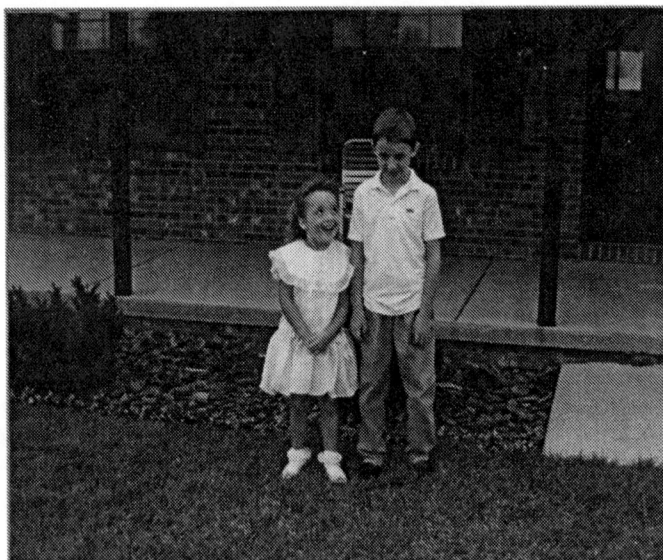

Brent and Grace all dressed up for church

CHAPTER 4
STARTING SCHOOL AND BEYOND

When Brent was four years old, I put him in a Co-op nursery school. I wanted him to get used to a school setting before he started kindergarten. There were about 20 kids in his class. He attended twice a week for two hours. Due to it being a Co-op school, I had to work twice a month in his class. I'm so glad I was able to do this, because I got to see him interact with his teacher as well as the other students. He did really well. He was able to stay on task and listen to the teacher most of the time.

At playtime, the boys would run around acting goofy, jumping on things and rolling around on the ground. The girls would sit and watch the boys. I often wondered what the girls were thinking about as they watched the boys.

I will never forget Brent's first day of kindergarten. He was really excited about riding the bus. I was afraid he would get lost from the bus to his classroom so we went to the school a few days ahead of time to make sure he knew where to go. My mom came over to watch him get on the bus, and to stay with Grace while I went to the school to make sure he got to his room OK.

(Do you think I was over-protective or something?) I stood by the entrance of the school and watched as Brent got off the bus and walked to his classroom. He didn't even notice me standing there. Brent did a wonderful job, he got off the bus and walked straight to his new classroom.

Brent loved school. He rarely gave me a hard time about going. The only year that he didn't like was 4th grade. He loved his teacher, but she got sick late in the school year and had to go through chemo. He was given a long-term substitute teacher that he didn't like. The teacher was very strict. Brent did better with a teacher that allowed a little breathing room. He said he was not going to school, and that his new teacher was the devil! That was a long few months!

When Brent was in 5th grade, he started getting into trouble. He was playing with matches and set a friend's bunk bed on fire. He also set fire to some debris at a construction site.

Jason took him to the fire department for a stern lecture. They also had him watch a video for at risk children. He also had to work two weekends at the police auction. That was the last time I ever had any problems with him regarding fires.

In 6th grade, Brent started middle school and it was very hard for him. He loved switching classes, but he couldn't keep up with the homework. I remember many nights sitting at the kitchen table helping him with his homework.

This is also the year of what I call the flood. Jason and I split up, and it had a devastating effect on the entire family. Grace, Brent, and I moved into an apartment.

The only one I could afford was not in the same school district that he was attending. I would take Brent to my parents' house at night, and my mom would take him to the bus stop at our old house in the morning. In the afternoon, I would meet him at the bus stop and take him home. We did this for six months. I was able to find an apartment that was on the bus route for 7th grade.

CHAPTER 5
TIM

Tim came into our lives when Brent was six years old. He was a friend of the family and we saw him on a weekly basis.

As the years went by, Tim and I ended up divorced from our spouses. We started seeing each other in 1997, and were married in May of 1999. Tim is the love of my life, my soul mate. Tim says that God put us together, and I agree. We have made God the foundation of our marriage and our home. We live by His principles, and He blesses us daily beyond anything we could ever imagine.

Tim has been an awesome stepfather to my children, as well as a wonderful father to his own son, Tommy. He has a ton of energy and is involved in many activities. My children were able to go places and do things that I never dreamed they would be able to do. Tim has taken Grace to several Nascar races. We went as a family to a Nascar race as well. Tim bought a jet boat that we enjoy taking to the lake. We bought a cabin up north in Houghton Lake. We enjoy spending summer and winter weekends there. Tim is an avid snowmobiler, and bought all the kids their own snowmobiles.

Life with Tim is always an adventure!

Tim managed a collision repair center for several years before buying his own shop.

Brent worked for Tim after school and on weekends.

He would clean the shop and help with light bodywork. Brent learned so much working for Tim.

Tim bought Brent a used Chevy S10 truck. Tim thought working on the truck would keep Brent focused on something positive. Once they had the bodywork done, they put a custom paint job on it. Once it was finished, they took it to car shows. It was really sharp and got a lot of attention. After owning it for several years, Brent sold it to a man that was going to drive it to Mexico. He would leave it there with his family and drive it when he went there to visit.

My mother says that Tim was Brent's angel, and I agree. God knew that he needed direction and love. Tim came into his life just at the right time. He was able to help Brent turn things around for a few years. I will be forever grateful to Tim for the unselfish love he gave to my dear son, Brent.

CHAPTER 6
GOD

J esus Christ is the Lord and Savior of my life.
I was raised in a Lutheran Church in Ypsilanti, Michigan.

My mother took us to church every Sunday. We would pick my maternal grandmother up on the way. After church, we would go to the donut shop. We would eat donuts and visit with my grandmother. This is such a wonderful memory for me.

When I was a teenager, I went out in the world and did things that I shouldn't have done. Thankfully, I didn't stay out there long. After Brent was born, I returned and I have served God every day since.

I raised Brent and Grace in the church the same way I was raised. We attended the Lutheran church until 1991, when my grandmother passed away.

Brent participated in the yearly Christmas plays. His first play was at three years old. Brent was very nervous about it. I had him dressed in a tan suit with a brown tie. Because Brent was so little, he was in the front row as the children were singing Christmas songs. He took the corner of his suit and started rolling it all the way up to his chin. Everyone was chuckling, it was so cute!

He took first communion classes in the 4th grade and then was able to participate in communion during services.

From age 12-14, he went through their catechism program.

My mother took him to the catechism classes every Thursday night for two years. This was a huge commitment for her and I'm very grateful that she did this for Brent.

He had to do some service work as part of the catechism requirement. He chose to work at the weekly meal the church provided for the needy. The Sunday he was confirmed, both my mother and I were in tears. We were so proud of him!

When he got older, he still helped in the church. My mom is very involved and helps with the coffee hour after church. Brent would also help. When he was older and lived in Green Bay, he would come back to Michigan for a visit and go to church with his grandmother.

Once my grandmother passed away, I decided to look for a new church. I tried several churches until I found a Freewill Baptist Church in Ypsilanti. I just loved it there. They had wonderful singers and the pastor preached from the bible, which I liked. We participated in the Christmas plays and I taught Sunday school there. Brent would attend both churches.

A few years later, the GM plant closed and many of the church members relocated to Texas. Brent was becoming a teenager and getting into trouble, and I knew I needed to get him into a church that had a good youth group.

I started searching for a new church and found a Church of God in Ypsilanti. The youth pastors were dynamic. They were on fire for God, and the kids just loved them.

I stayed there until 2000, when Tim and I started looking for a new church home.

We started attending an Assembly of God church in Ypsilanti. Tim, Tommy and I still attend this church today. I teach Sunday school and just love it. We have a bus ministry and we pick up needy children. I'm so thankful that I can tell them about the good news of God. That He is there for them, and He will see them through any situation. I have birthday parties for them with cupcakes and presents. I also have special activities on holidays.

They all get a candy bar to take home with them if they have been good during class. So far, no one has acted up enough to not get one! I have threatened them a few times! When the kids move up to an older classroom, a lot of them still stop by my class for a candy bar and a hug. Working with children is my calling from God, and I'm so thankful that I'm able to do it. My Pastor is awesome, and also has a calling for the children. We are in the process of renovating a large building. It will house our church, along with a full-size basketball court. We feel we need to reach the teenagers in the area, and this is one way we can do that.

Tim and I bring two girls to church with us. One is in my class, and her sister is my helper. I have watched both of them grow in the Lord, and it warms my heart that we are able to bring them.

When Brent came back to live with us before his death, we went to church every Sunday. He would either go with us or with my mom.

He was struggling with his addiction, but I knew if he could connect with God, he would be OK.

During that time, a woman I had never met started coming to our church. She carried a briefcase and I often wondered what she had inside it. She would sit in the pew directly in front of us. She was very anointed and prayed beautifully during the service. The last Sunday I saw her, she turned around and lay her hands on Brent and started to pray for him. I'm not sure what she prayed, because I was too far down the pew to hear her. The bible says in Hebrews 13:2, "Be not forgetful to entertain strangers: for thereby some have entertained angels unawares." I'm not sure if she was an angel sent by God, or if God led her to our church for Brent.

Since the day she prayed for Brent, I haven't seen her again.

One morning, I was feeling very sad that Brent was alone when he died. I started reading my bible and I turned to Luke 16:19-31. The story is about Lazarus the beggar. He had a very hard life. He was sick, with sores all over his body. He would lay at the rich man's gate and beg for crumbs. When he died, the bible says he was carried to heaven by angels. God showed me that Brent was not alone that night; the angels were there with him and carried him to heaven.

I don't know exactly what happened to him that night. I'm assuming that God spoke to him on or shortly before that night, and he surrendered his heart to God. Brent led a very difficult life. He ran the streets and did things that he should not have done. I believe his lifestyle could have led him to hell, but we serve a God who gives us grace. I believe that God gave Brent grace and took him home to be with Him in heaven.

As hard as it is to not have Brent here with me, I'm comforted by knowing that he is in heaven. There, he is no longer tormented by the disease of alcoholism and drug addiction. His body no longer craves those things. He is safe and warm in God's loving hands.

If you are reading this book right now, and you don't have a personal relationship with God, I urge you to ask God to come into your heart. I also urge you to find a good bible-based church where you can grow spiritually. God is my strength. If I didn't have Him in my life, I would never have made it through this tragedy. He carries me when I cannot walk, and gives me courage to face each day.

CHAPTER 7
PRAYER

I heard a message preached at church called Prayer is Productive.

The bible tells us to pray without ceasing; I Thessalonians 5:17.

Having a drug-addicted child motivated me to pray without ceasing. It was tormenting to watch my son make horrible decisions, which many times left him in dire circumstances. If it wasn't for my faith in God and the knowledge that He would take care of Brent, I don't think I could have made it.

Many times, my prayers were frantic. It's awful not knowing where your child is, or if they are OK. I would say, "Dear Lord, please protect Brent. Keep him safe and help him find recovery."

I would also say prayers for myself. I had many sleepless nights when I didn't know where he was, or what he was doing. I would pray for God to give me peace so I could sleep.

Then, when he did get into trouble, I would pray for God to help us get through it.

When a person has an addiction, it runs their life. They do very dangerous things to get their drugs. They go places that would make a non-addicted person's skin crawl.

Many nights, Brent went to Detroit to get his drugs. He

also was jacked for his money several times. One night, he went and picked a guy up that told him he would take him to get some pot. Brent drove him around for a while, then the guy said, "OK, pull over here, and give me your money." He said, "I'll go in and get the drugs. If you go with me, they won't sell it to me."

Brent gave him the money and waited. The guy never came back. Brent went into the building and it was vacant. Thankfully, Brent didn't get hurt in that transaction, he only lost his money. Many nights, I worried that Brent would get killed in Detroit and I would never know what happened to him. Sometimes, I can't believe that Brent didn't sense the danger that he put himself in. When you are on drugs, it's like you have tunnel vision; the only thing you can think about is getting high. The danger doesn't even play into it.

I went to an open Alcoholics Anonymous speaker meeting one night. A recovering addict spoke about his drive to get drugs. He said he was walking in a bad part of town looking for someone to sell to him when a person came up and put a knife to his throat. He said, "Give me your money."

The addict said to the robber, "Hey man, do what you have to do, but hurry up."

He said he didn't care that he might get stabbed, all he cared about was for the guy to hurry up so he could go find some drugs.

CHAPTER 8
13 AND UP

B rent's first run-in with drugs occurred at the end of 6th grade. He bought some pot from someone at school and got caught. I was called to the school to pick him up. It was almost the last day of the school, so they were very lenient on him. They said due to the situation at home, and that it was the end of the school year, they were not going to punish him. He was very relieved. I was very angry!

I yelled at him at the top of my lungs all the way home.

He also got into trouble at the apartment complex we were living in. He stole a laptop from one of the workers. When I got home that night, there was a call from the office on my answering machine. They needed me to come down and talk to them about my son. The staff told me that Brent was seen near the office when the laptop disappeared, so they thought he had something to do with the theft. I went home to discuss this with him, but he was not there. I looked everywhere for the laptop and finally found it under his bed. I took it to the office.

The gentlemen that it belonged to was so relieved to have it back that he didn't press charges.

Brent knew he was in trouble and was nowhere to be found. It wasn't until midnight that Jason found him walking alongside a road. He knew I was furious, so he spent the night with Jason.

I had no idea what to do with that kid.

In 9th grade, we moved to Livonia for one year. He loved it there. It was a big city with a lot going on. He was never home. He took a job at a party store, and from what I understand, he would sneak beer. He hooked up with a friend from school that also worked at the party store. When they were together, they were usually up to no good.

In 10th grade, we moved to Belleville. I purchased a very nice mobile home.

This is where Brent's drug career really went into high gear. He hooked up with a kid that was into a lot of trouble. At school, he managed to only pass a gym class the entire year.

He bought a gun at a crack house and was discharging it in our neighborhood and got caught.

I got a phone call from the Sumpter Township Police Department while I was at work. I didn't even know where the police station was. I had just started dating Tim, so I called him for directions. The juvenile police officer told me that Brent was in a lot of trouble. I asked the officer if I needed to get him a lawyer, and he said no. He said that Brent would have a court appointed juvenile representative assigned to his case. The gun that he bought was stolen, so we had to wait and see if any crimes were connected to the gun. If the gun had been used in a crime, Brent would be charged with the crime, whether he did it or not. We had to wait a week for the results of the search. The gun came back clean, which meant Brent was only charged with discharging it. We were both very relieved.

The city of Belleville is in Wayne County, and Wayne County's court system is in Detroit.

Brent had a court date for the firearms charge, so off to Detroit we went. When we got to the court building, we were treated like criminals. We waited in line to go through the metal detectors. Once we were through, a lady yelled at me to put my purse on the table. She turned it upside down and everything started falling all over the table and to the floor. She just stood there and looked at me like I was an idiot for bringing the purse in the first place. Here I was, trying to grab everything that was falling to the floor, and lay it back on the table. She yelled for the next person, so I figured she was done with me, and I put everything back in my purse and moved on.

The courthouse was packed with people. Most of the people didn't have their children with them; they were being brought in from detention centers.

I didn't know what to do about Brent and his problems. The police officer told me that Brent needed to be in detention. We waited two hours to see the judge. I kept praying for God to give me a sign as to what to do.

We met with his juvenile representative, she was a lady in her 50s. She was very sharply dressed in a blue skirt and jacket. She read his case and said, "Do you want to take him home with you?"

I answered, "I don't know what to do."

She said, "We'll see what the judge says."

Once we were seated in the courtroom, immediately the police officer stood up and said, "Brent is a danger to society, and he should be locked up!"

Brent's rep stood up and said, "This is his first offence, which does not warrant detention!"

The judge looked at me and asked, "Are you willing to take him home with you and work with a social worker?"

I said, "Yes, I will."

The judge pounded her gavel on the desk and said, "I am placing Brent Anthony Legault on house arrest and in the custody of his mother. I am ordering a case study to be done, with the results sent to me once it is completed."

After that, she stood up and walked out of the chambers. I breathed a sigh of relief and thanked God for handling the situation for me. What I have learned to do with problems is give them to God and ask for his guidance. That's exactly what I did and it all worked out. I was so very thankful to be taking him home with me. I didn't want him to go to a detention center in Detroit.

Tim and I decided Brent needed to change schools. He had practically failed 10th grade, and the kids he was running with were not good influences. Tim got him enrolled in the Milan School district. The day before Brent was to start Milan, Tim came over to my house and told Brent to pack an overnight bag.

Brent asked, "Why?"

Tim said, "Because you're coming with me, I have you starting Milan school in the morning."

Brent said, "Oh man."

Tim said, "Get going." Brent got up and got packed. This turned out to be a very positive move. Tim would drop him off at school in the morning and pick him up from school in the afternoon. After school, Brent would work at the shop with Tim. There wasn't a lot of time for Brent to get into trouble.

We met with the social worker three times. She came to my house once and we went to her office twice. She was a very nice lady. She recommended that Brent be put into treatment for his drug and alcohol addiction, and be on probation for a year and a half.

This started the ball rolling for Brent's recovery.

CHAPTER 9
TENNESSEE TRIP

Tim and I took our first family vacation to Gatlin-burg, Tenn. over the Christmas holiday in 1999.

We drove my red aerostar van. We stopped in Georgia for one night on the way down. They had a heated indoor pool, and we all went swimming. There was only one other person in the pool so it felt like we had the place almost to ourselves. For some reason, Grace, Tommy, and I got sick on that trip. We had flu-like symptoms. First it was Grace, then me and then Tommy. Brent slept on the floor on the other side of the room with blankets over his head so he wouldn't get sick. He said he didn't want to breath in our germs! It worked because he didn't get sick.

One night, Grace was sick and was sleeping on the floor by the bathroom. Tommy got up to go to the bath-room and then lay next to Grace on the floor. He knew that he was sleeping by her when he went to bed, so when he came out of the bathroom and saw her on the floor, he lay down next to her. It was so cute! Another night, Grace was dreaming and she stood up, started waving her arms, and said "Lion King." Tim asked her what she was doing and she just kept saying, "Lion King!" He lay her back down and told her to go to sleep. It was very funny. We still tease her about it!

There was a Christian youth conference going on when

we got down there, and it was packed with teens. The boys were chasing after Grace, and the girls were chasing after Brent. We couldn't go down the street without a girl coming up to Brent and talking to him. It was crazy! Grace loved it; she and Tommy would walk around the hotel while she checked the guys out. They were in the elevator with two other boys when Tommy looked up at them and said to Grace, "Do you think they're cute?" She was embarrassed and told Tommy to shut up! Needless to say, she brought him back to the room and left him with us!

We had a suite with two bedrooms back to back. The windows faced another set of windows on the other side of the hotel. Grace was in one window and the boys were hooting and hollering across the hotel from the other set of windows. Tim went into the other room and shook his fist at the boys, so they stopped. Grace came out wondering why the boys went away. Tim and I laughed, but didn't tell her that Tim was scaring them off!

Brent took off on us one night, and was gone for hours. He later told Tim he was getting drunk with some girls. When Tim went looking for him, he saw him walking down the sidewalk. He rolled the window down and told him to get in the car. Tim was very angry.

Brent did his usual, "What?" He always said that when he was in trouble. "What, what did I do?" He also said later he was high the entire trip. That explains why he didn't fight with his sister like he usually did.

CHAPTER 10
MUSIC

When Brent was ten years old, he took piano lessons. The lessons were once a week for an hour at a time. Between the lessons, he would practice at his Grandma Patty's house. She had a beautiful oak piano that sat in the foyer of her home. She would spend hours with him practicing his lesson. She was very patient and kind. I believe those hours spent with her helped blossom the love he had for music. Brent and his grandma had a very special relationship. Brent was the first grandchild, and she always made sure he felt loved.

She would make the special foods he liked. He loved candy, but it made him hyper so I limited how much he could have. His grandma always had candy in dishes throughout the house. When he came home from her house, he would be very hyper. One day, she cleaned behind an armoire in her bedroom and found hundreds of candy wrappers. Brent would eat the candy and throw the wrappers behind the armoire so no one knew how much he was eating.

As an adult, Brent's favorite musical group was the White Stripes. Whenever he got a new CD, he would come home and yell for Tommy. They would go down to the basement and listen to the CD with Brent's headphones. Brent would listen with one headphone, and Tommy would listen with the other one.

Tim bought me a baby grand piano for my birthday one year. I always wanted to take music lessons, but never did. Brent would play the piano for hours. He would also sing along, which made Tommy mad. Tommy would yell at Brent to keep it down, he was trying to watch TV. Brent would just play and sing louder!

We used to have a man named Bob play the piano at our church. He would make the keys rock. I would sit in church and feel like I was in heaven when he played. Bob left our church to marry a woman in another country. Unfortunately, Brent was unable to hear him play. When Brent started playing our piano, it sounded like Bob.

It was like their fingers were anointed by God, and would flow over the keys. I would be in the kitchen fixing dinner sometimes when Brent was playing. It warmed my heart to hear him play so beautifully.

I asked Brent one day if he wanted to play the piano at church. He said he would really like to play the drums. He said he wanted a set of his own to practice on before he would play anywhere else. I was planning on buying him a drum set for Christmas the year he passed on. I know that he is up in heaven playing the piano or the drums for God, and some day when I get there, I will be able to hear him play once again.

CHAPTER 11
THREE FRIENDS

When we lived in Belleville, Brent had 2 friends that he hung out with. Believe me, they were not kids that I approved of. Once Brent hooked up with them, he started doing a lot of really bad things. He was selling drugs and breaking into cars. Once he got into treatment, he shared with Tim and I some of the things he had done. I knew he was selling drugs, but I didn't know about the other things he was doing.

One night, the police knocked on my door with the drug-sniffing dog. There had been an armed robbery of a woman in the area. The description from the woman sounded like Brent and his two friends. They searched my entire house with the dog. Once the dog got to the heat vent in Brent's room, it started scratching and barking. The officer reached down and found a gun along with a dinner plate with some kind of white residue on it. Brent said the gun was not his; it was someone else's and he was holding it for them.

The robbery had taken place on Friday night, and I had dropped Brent off at my parents' house for the weekend. The police talked to my mom about Brent being there and she said he was. Charges were never pressed against Brent for the robbery or for hiding the gun.

There was a police officer that lived in our neighbor-hood. He would patrol at night. Many nights, Brent said he had to hide from the officer. One night, the officer had him get in the car and patrol with him. Brent said he thought for sure he was busted. I think the officer was smarter than Brent thought. He was watching him and the other two kids, and as soon as he needed them for something, he could coerce them into talking.

Grace's friend, Abby, lived with her mom and dad one street over. Her dad was a police officer. We went to a Christmas party years later, and met up with them. He told us that one of Brent's friends was wanted for rape and robbery. The other boy was found at the side of the road dead, with a needle in his arm. He died of a drug overdose. I always thought that out of the three kids, Brent was the one that would make it. I was wrong, none of the boys made it.

When you are caught up in the drug world, it is very hard to make it out.

God and Alcoholics Anonymous are the only ways that I have ever seen anyone get out.

The person has to really want to change their life. A significant life event must take place to get their attention. They either get into a lot of trouble, or their family falls apart. They might have a near-death experience that gets their attention. One thing the family will do is bail them out of every scrape so they never feel the pain of their circumstances. The best thing the family can do if they end up in jail is to leave them there. Make them face their problems. Pain motivates. Pain motivates the family members to try something different, and pain motivates the user to try and get their life back in order. It's extremely hard to watch a loved one suffer, but until they hit bottom hard enough, they will continue down the road to destruction, taking everyone who cares for them down with them.

CHAPTER 12
DARKNESS

When Brent was 15, he started to dabble in the occult. I didn't know about it until one evening, the police showed up at my door looking for him. While searching the house, the police found a paper with the name Lucifer on it. The name was in the middle of the paper with circles around it. Around the circles were writing that said, "I want to be like you."

The officer was appalled and threw the paper on the coffee table. He kept yelling at Brent about it. He said, "So you want to be like him, so you want to have his powers." Brent just sat there saying nothing. I sat on the couch in shock. I had no idea he was into that.

After Brent died, I googled his name to see if it would come up on any websites. It came up on a site for the occult. Brent had joined a pagan online group, and the last time he signed on was Sept. 10th, 2005. His profile said he wanted to get with people who had the same beliefs as he did. The site is based in Green Bay, Wisconsin. The people have meetings there. The site had a picture of Brent that I had never seen before. He was looking serious and his eyes were staring down. The picture gave me the creeps, it made him look evil.

When I saw this, I was in shock. He had been going to church with us since August, and he was going behind our backs to do this stuff. No wonder he was so tormented.

The bible says you cannot serve two masters. I have a sign on the wall at my house that says, "But as for me and my house, we will serve the Lord," Joshua 24:15.

My very special Christian friend, Ysabelle, knew that we were battling with Brent's addiction problems, so she told me to start doing a family devotion together at night. Every night, we would read from a family devotion book and then read passages from the bible that pertained to the devotion for that day. After, we would hold hands and pray the Lord's Prayer. Many nights, Brent was high. Brent was stuck in two worlds. One was the Christian world that his family was involved in, and the other one was very dark. I knew he was high many nights that we were doing the devotion, but I never stopped trying to reach him.

Tim's birthday party,
Brent was using drugs heavily that year

CHAPTER 13
MERCY HOUSE

While attending the Church of God in Ypsilanti, Tim and I met our dear friends, Celon and Betty. They are very special to us. I call them my spiritual mother and father. Betty has a passion for feeding the hungry. She and Celon have been involved in many outreach programs throughout the years. When we first met them, they were involved in an outreach ministry in Detroit called Mercy House. Once a month, they would go with the church to preach and feed the hungry. Betty is an awesome cook! Every meal she serves is fit for a king. She says she cooks as if she is cooking for Jesus! She was in charge of purchasing the food, cooking it, and taking it to Detroit.

Tim and I got involved and started going to her house to help prepare the food. It was an awesome experience. We would make enough food to feed 100 people. So many miracles took place in their home while we were cooking. One time, we were making potatoes and God multiplied it. We used the same amount of ingredients that we had used before, but this time we had an extra pan of potatoes. It was a good thing, because that night we fed over 100 people. God knew the amount of food we would need and he provided it.

Many of the people would comment on how the food was prepared just like their grandma used to make. A lot of them knew what week we would be there, and they waited anxiously to see what we had prepared for them.

Brent went with us twice. He helped with the set up and clean up. He was very touched by how needy the people were. It was a moving experience for him. I'm so thankful that he also had a soft spot for the needy, just like we did.

One night, Betty and Celon's son, Michael (who is a preacher), came and preached the word. It was awesome to hear him preach.

There was a lady there that had been severely beaten. She sat in a chair down from me, and leaned her swollen face against a post. We gently lay our hands on her and prayed. I'm not sure if she was able to eat any food that night. She came because she knew she would be safe and no one would judge her. We loved her unconditionally. I will surely never forget that woman.

Another time in the middle of winter, a couple came with a small baby. We let them stay in the building while we were cleaning up. It broke all our hearts when it was time for them to leave and go back into the cold. We all prayed that they would find a warm and safe place to stay. A few months later, they came back, we were so happy to see them.

I truly believe that God will bless you so you can be a blessing to others. I always think, "What would Jesus do?" Jesus fed the multitudes. He gave them nourishment for their bodies, and spiritual food for their souls. I believe that is what God expects us to do also.

CHAPTER 14
TREATMENT

When Brent was 16 years old, he went into an outpatient drug treatment program in Plymouth. There were 20 kids in the program with him. He attended three times a week for two-hour sessions. Brent was not driving at the time, so Tim, my dad and I would get him there and back. It was a 30-40 minute drive one way. I will be forever grateful to Tim and my dad for taking the time out of their busy lives to help Brent. I couldn't have done it without them.

When my dad took him, they would go down the street to an ice cream parlor for ice cream after his session. They both enjoyed their time together. My parents were always very involved in Brent's life.

Brent responded positively to treatment right away, and was able to stop using.

He knew he had to give weekly urine tests, which kept him on his toes. He also attended five Alcoholic Anonymous meetings a week.

Brent started to care about his appearance. When he left for school in the morning, Tim would say he was looking good and smelling good. He started dating a cheerleader, and he was praying at the flagpole every morning before school. Our home life calmed down. We weren't waiting for the police to arrive, or for a phone call telling us he was in trouble.

Brent took driver's training, and was able to get his license. He went to the prom with the cheerleader he was dating. We had a black Explorer at the time, which Brent asked to borrow. Tim said, "No way you have to drive the Escort." He was mad! He cleaned the Escort up, washed and waxed it. I don't think it ever looked that good!

He brought his date over to the house for pictures. They looked wonderful!

Tim said to be home at midnight, but I doubt he was.

Things were looking up!

CHAPTER 15
ALANON

I grew up in an alcoholic home. My father is the alcoholic. He went into treatment in May 1985. I'm so very proud of him. He has helped hundreds of people throughout his years in recovery. He is a very caring and compassionate man. He also works his recovery program and when he leads a meeting, it's no nonsense. If you want help, it would be a good idea to do what he does and go where he goes. One of the slogans of Alcoholics Anonymous is stick with the winners. That's what you do when you go to meetings and spend your idle time with other people in recovery.

My mother started going to Alanon in 1984. It helped her deal with my dad's problems, and was the catalyst for my father going into treatment.

My father went into a local treatment center in Ypsilanti for 28 days. It was very hard on all of us when he went in. Brent was very close to his grandpa and to not see him every day was hard.

I used to take Brent to McDonalds to play and have a snack at night in the winter. I always had to keep him busy. We were at McDonalds one night, and I saw the van from the treatment center pull up to the curb. I looked and my dad was in the van. I grabbed Brent and ran outside. My dad saw us and he came to the van door. I'm so thankful that the man driving the van let my dad get out and give us a hug and talk for a few minutes. Brent was so excited, he was jumping up and down. I was, of course, crying. I'm known in the family for being the crier! When it was time for them to leave, we stood on the curb and waved until the bus was out of sight. I call that a God moment. God makes it possible for everyone involved to be at the right place at the right time. Brent and I were so very happy to have gotten to see him.

They had a family day at the treatment center. I really didn't want to go, but I felt obligated. My sister and I went to one room and my mother went somewhere else. It was a classroom setting with a chalkboard and chairs set up in a row with no desks. We went in and sat down and listened. I really couldn't get what the guy was saying. He said something about it being a disease, and that once you have it, you can never use again. He said it was a family disease in that it affects everyone in the family.

I was thinking, "What's he talking about, what am I doing here. I no longer live with my parents, I have my own life. I live on my own, work and have a child." I just didn't get it. I remember going into the bathroom with my sister and I said, "What are we doing here?"

She said, "Dad's an alcoholic."

I said, "What?"

Lynn said again, "Dad's an alcoholic." I just couldn't comprehend what she was saying.

All my life, everyone was saying there was nothing wrong in our house. Sure, dad drinks, but all dads drink. I felt very confused, even off balance. Everything that I had thought during my entire life, was being challenged. I didn't like it at all.

I went back to the center a few times to eat lunch with my dad, and I took Brent with me. Brent loved seeing his grandpa. He would climb into the chair next to his grandpa and just smile. I saw one of the guys I went to school with there. He came over and talked to me. He said that he was going to be going into long-term treatment soon. I said I hope it went well. I saw him about four years ago, and he didn't look well. He looked like Brent did for so many years; very skinny and malnourished. He said hi to me and I said hi back. He didn't stop and talk, so I assumed he was still out there using. It's very sad.

I started attending Alanon meetings in the fall of 1988. I tell people that my mother hit me over the head and dragged me to a meeting, which is somewhat correct. She bugged me for a while about going, so to get her off my back, I decided to go. I felt at home at the very first meeting. Everyone was very kind, and it was a safe place to share my feelings. I continue to go to meetings because it helps me. I have learned tools to help me deal with the effects the disease has had on my life. I encourage anyone who has been or is currently affected by the disease to give Alanon a try. It has saved my life many times over.

CHAPTER 16
DRIVING

Brent took driver's training when he was 16. He was doing well with his drug treatment so we decided to reward him by letting him learn to drive. He took the classes in Ann Arbor, and once he was able to drive with a parent, Tim worked with him daily.

One day after his session at the treatment center, I asked if he wanted to drive. He said, "Sure." He got in the driver's seat and we headed out. He didn't look closely going out of the parking lot and sped out in front of a car. I yelled at him and he pulled the car over. He said, "I'm not driving with you in the car any more." I thought to myself, good! He never drove with me again. I felt bad for Tim because that meant he was left with the responsibility of teaching him.

Brent was a terrible driver. Many people that saw him on the road agreed.

Tim tells of the time he took Brent to his driving test with the state. Brent sat in the driver's seat, the man administering the test sat in the passenger seat, and Tim sat in the back. Brent was leaning over with his elbow on the armrest and only one hand on the steering wheel as they headed out. At the stop sign, the man said, "Mr. Legault, we can do one of two things. You can either sit up straight and put both hands on the wheel, or you can come back in a year to take the test." Tim said Brent immediately sat up straight and put both hands on the wheel. Tim chuckled to himself. Tim still laughs today when he tells the story. Amazingly, Brent passed his driving test. I told him that he had Tim to thank for it.

One afternoon, my entire family met for my Aunt Joanne's birthday at a restaurant in Ann Arbor.

We were all in the parking lot gathering together when a car came speeding around the corner, literally jumping the curb and going on two wheels. Guess who was in the car? None other than Brent! My Uncle Alton and Aunt Joanne owned an insurance company at the time, and my mother was one of their agents. They were all thankful they did not have Brent insured with them!

Another time, my mom was on her way home and she saw Brent's car ahead of her. He was holding up three lanes of traffic. He wanted to turn left, but he was in the wrong lane. She said people were honking and yelling. She just shook her head.

Brent was very hard on the cars he drove, he would tear them up.

Brent and his friend were on the back roads doing I don't know what, and his clutch went out. He called Tim to come and get him. The next day, Tim was looking at the car and found the clutch broken into pieces. It was a five-speed, and Brent must have been beating on the car to have it break like that. The guys in the shop said they had never seen a clutch broken that bad. They all teased Brent for a long time over that one!

Brent had a K car that he hated, but it ran great. He wanted a newer vehicle, but because he was so hard on cars, Tim wouldn't buy him one. Finally, I got tired of looking at it parked in front of the house so I talked Tim into getting Brent a newer car.

Brent used shoe polish to write For Sale on the car, and also put the asking price of $100. He was on his way home one day and two ladies followed him, I'm not sure how they were able to keep up with him! They both wanted the car and ended up arguing over it. I'm not sure how Brent decided who he would sell it to.

CHAPTER 17
NIC

B rent and Nic met at Milan High School when they were in the 11th grade.

They became fast friends. If you saw Brent, you knew Nic was not far behind. They had a lot of the same qualities. They were full of energy, smart and charismatic. They were well-liked by everyone. They also seemed to get into trouble. They would leave school at lunchtime and have a hard time making their way back.

One of the funniest stunts they pulled was when Tim and I were on vacation.

They bought some firecrackers. I never really got the real story so I will tell what I know about the incident. They were driving down the road and lit one of the firecrackers. Before they could throw it out the window, it dropped on the driver's seat. They both bailed out of the car as it was still going down the road. Brent took the car down to Tim's shop the next day and was frantically trying to clean all the burn marks. Tim's employees told him that he was going to be very mad when he found out.

A few weeks later, Tim was with Brent in the car and he noticed some burn marks on the seat. Tim said, "Brent, what happened to your seat?"

Brent answered, "Nic dropped a cigarette."

Tim said, "No, that's not what happened." Brent stuck

to his story until a few years later, when he fessed up about what really happened.

After they graduated from high school, Nic moved to Minnesota to live with his dad, and Brent moved to Green Bay, Wisconsin. They still kept in touch. Nic came to Michigan and stayed with us during Brent's funeral. He also met us at our cabin for a weekend.

It was bitter sweet. I was happy to see Nic, but sad that Brent was no longer with us.

CHAPTER 18
KELLY

B rent and Kelly met at a local college frat party. I didn't meet her for a few months, but when I did, she said to me, "You don't look psychotic to me." I guess Brent told her I was psycho.

When you live with someone who actively uses drugs and alcohol, you can act a little crazy at times. I only wanted what was best for Brent, and when he was using, I knew he was destroying himself. His drug use bothered me a lot more than it bothered him.

Kelly was the love of Brent's life. They were very compatible. Brent was very bright and so is Kelly. They would have many interesting conversations, which Brent loved.

He was up on all the latest news and also loved to talk about any number of topics.

After Brent graduated from high school, he moved to Green Bay, Wisconsin to be with Kelly. She grew up there and it's where her family lives. Tim, Grace and I helped Brent pack his things for the move. He left a few days before we did. We rented a trailer to put everything in.

It was a long nine-hour drive. We had to go through Chicago. It was the first time I had been there.

We got to Chicago around 10:00 pm. I was sleeping in the front seat until I heard Tim yelling that we almost got hit by a car that swerved into our lane. He was pretty shook up. The traffic was just awful. We had to go through toll-booths and at each booth, they charged us a different rate. There is a different fee for a 1, 2 or 4 axle trailers. Tim started to get frustrated with the fees. One of the guys gave him some money back when Tim questioned him!

It was getting late so we decided to pull over and stay in a hotel near Six Flags. We were hungry so we went to a Little Caesar's restaurant and got a pizza, breadsticks, and pop to go. We were amazed that it cost under $10. It was so much cheaper than in Michigan. The next morning, we headed back out. We arrived at Brent and Kelly's apartment around 10:00 am. Kelly's mom was there, and Kelly intro-duced us. She was very nice. Brent had decided he was go-ing to work for an industrial construction company, so after we unpacked everything, we took him to Lowe's to get a tool belt and some tools. He worked one day and decided it wasn't for him!

We also went to K-marts and got some chairs for their dining room table.

That night, Kelly's parents had us over for dinner. Her mother was a very good cook. We were able to meet Kelly's dad, who was also very nice. Grace still gives me a hard time about what happened at dinner that night. She spilled some chocolate on her shirt and was trying to be discreet about it. I blurted out, "Grace, you spilled choco-late on your shirt." At that point, everyone looked at Grace and her shirt. She said she wanted to climb under the table. After dinner, we all went outside and said our goodbyes. It was very hard to leave Brent. We had been together for 19 years. This would be the first time we had ever been apart for any length of time. Grace and I cried all the way back to Michigan. I sat in the back seat so I could sleep. Grace was up front with Tim. She would cry for a while and when she stopped crying, I would start. It was just awful.

There was some excitement on the way home. It was after midnight and two cars went screaming by. It looked like one was chasing the other. Then further up the road, one of the cars had run off the road and the police were checking it out.

Thankfully, we got home safely.

Brent with the love of his life, Kelly

Brent, Barb and Tim on a visit to Green Bay

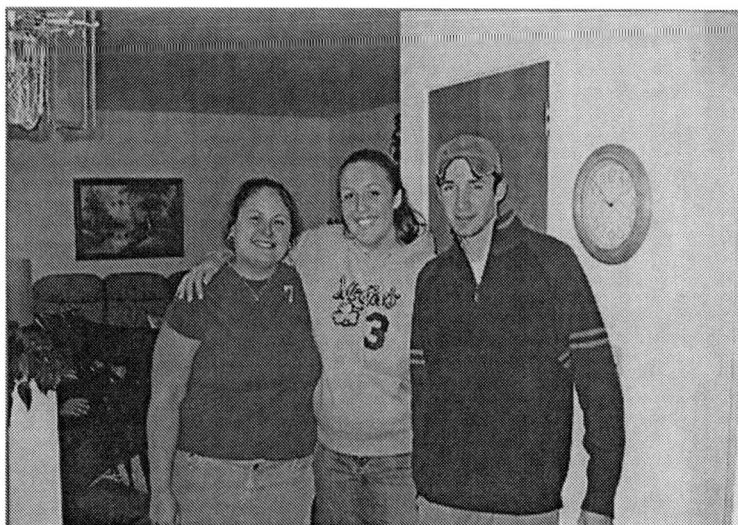
Kelly, Grace and Brent Christmas 2004

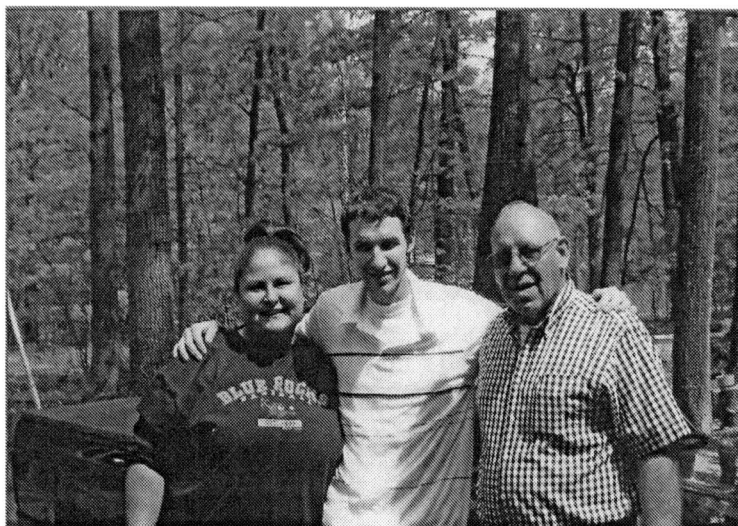
Kelly, Brent and Grandpa Herb at the cabin

Brent and Tommy at the cabin playing catch

Brent having fun on the Harley

CHAPTER 19
COLLEGE

Brent attended the Northeast Wisconsin Technical College for one year. He studied computer programming. One weekend, he met us at our cabin. He had his schoolbooks with him and he was showing me the work he was doing at school. It looked really hard to me! Brent was not having any trouble figuring the problems out. He was very smart. Even as a small boy, he was always able to catch on quick to things. He would get bored at school if he wasn't challenged.

CHAPTER 20
AUBREY

Kelly worked at a day care center. She was assigned to care for the babies.

She became very attached to a child named Aubrey. She started caring for her when she was six weeks old. Kelly would also baby-sit for her on the weekends.

Brent loved Aubrey and she loved Brent as well. Kelly and Brent would take her fun places. They fed the ducks at the park and went to the zoo.

Brent never had any children of his own, but I feel that being with Aubrey was the closest he got to having his own child. He would talk very lovingly about her.

Just like a parent would share the new things that their child had learned, Brent would do the same with Aubrey. He was so excited when she started walking and talking.

One time, they were at the park feeding the ducks and she got bit. Brent was so upset. He knew she would be afraid to go back and feed them again.

Today, when Kelly sees her, Aubrey asks where Brent is and Kelly tells her that he is in heaven with papa.

CHAPTER 21
SUICIDE ATTEMPT

B rent and Kelly broke up in April 2005 after being together for 5 years. It was very hard on both of them, because they still loved each other very much. Brent's using was getting worse, and it was hard for Kelly to deal with.

The day of April 14, 2005 will be forever etched in my mind. I had just gotten home from work and was talking to Tim. We were also trying to decide what we were going to do for dinner. The phone rang and it was Kelly. She was very upset and said that she didn't know where Brent was, and there was blood all over the apartment. I asked her what the name of the nearest hospital was. I was about to call information to get the phone number when the phone rang.

It was a lady calling from Wisconsin. She asked me what my name was and I told her. She told me she was a social worker and my son was in the hospital for a suicide attempt. I asked her if he was OK, and she said yes, but it was a very serious attempt (he slit his wrists) and I should get there as soon as possible.

I told her I would come, but it would take nine hours by car. I told her I would call the airlines to see if I could get a flight out. She said she would call me back in one hour.

I asked if I could talk to Brent and she said no. I was in a panic. I knew he was having some depression issues surrounding his breakup with Kelly, but I really didn't think he would do this.

I called my parents and they came over right away. They said they would stay with Grace and Tommy. I called the airlines and the first available flight would be at 10:00 pm. The cost would be $800 each! I could not believe the price. When I flew Brent and Kelly in for Christmas, it was $120 each. I even told the airline agent it was an emergency and that my son was in the hospital, but she didn't care. I talked it over with Tim and we both agreed we needed to get there as soon as we could, so I booked it. By that time, it was close to 7:00 pm. The social worker called back and I told her our plans. She said that we would not be able to see Brent until the next day. They were assessing his situation and deciding on a treatment plan. She said to call her in the morning. Tim called Grace and told her to come home. She was devastated when she heard the news. I got us packed and we headed for the airport.

Thankfully, we live 20 minutes away from the Detroit Metro Airport, so the drive wasn't even an issue. At the airport, we had a 45-minute wait until we could board our plane.

Tim called his boss to tell him what was going on. I had called my boss Kevin from home. I was so thankful to work for such an understanding person. He said to take as much time as I needed and to not worry about work, they would be OK. God puts angels in our lives to help us, and Kevin is one of those angels. I don't think he will ever know how much I appreciate the compassion and support he has given me throughout the years. Tim called his good friend Bill and told him. He was so very understanding. He and his wife, Rhonda, are true friends. Tim calls Bill his brother-in-law, and I call Rhonda another one of my angels. We are truly blessed to have them in our lives.

I was having an anxiety attack sitting there waiting to

board the plane. I knew Brent was going to be OK, but not being able to talk to him or see him was very hard. I, of course, was thinking about the worst that could happen. I started crying and it was hard to stop. Thankfully, it only takes 45 minutes to get to the Green Bay airport. We rented a car and found a hotel.

To my surprise, I was able to sleep five hours. When I woke up, I looked at the clock and it said 5:00 am. I knew I couldn't call the social worker until 8:00 am so I turned the TV on to distract myself. At 8:00 am on the dot, I called the social worker. She said Brent was transferred to a mental hospital and said we could see him at 10:00 am. We showered, got some breakfast and went to the hospital.

The hospital was tucked in a valley next to a neighborhood. It wasn't very big, maybe three stories high. We parked and went in. Everything was locked down. We had to show ID and get badges just to get through the first door. The receptionist was very nice and gave us our badges then let us in. She said to go to the second floor and ring the bell.

Once we were through the security door and walking down the hall, I saw someone walking towards me. Before I could see who it was, Brent said, "Mom." I couldn't believe it was him; it didn't look like him. I could tell he had been through a lot. He was wearing a knit hat and some hospital scrubs. He didn't have any shoes on, only socks that the hospital had given him. His wrists were wrapped in bandages. As much as I was relieved to see him, my heart was also broken to see him in such a bad shape. He hugged Tim and I, and then said he had to go talk to someone. The nurse took us to a lounge area to talk. She had a daughter that had a drug problem so she understood our anguish.

They called us to a room to meet with a psychiatrist and counselor. Brent was also present. The counselor talked to Brent about what had happened, and then he asked Tim and

I what we wanted to see happen. Right away, I said, "I want Brent to fly back with us and go into treatment." As soon as Brent heard the word treatment, he started shaking his head no.

The counselor said, "OK, Brent what do you think should happen?"

Brent said, "I'm not going into treatment."

The counselor said, "OK, try not using drugs or alcohol for six months. You are going to be job hunting and almost all employers will ask for a drug screen, so it is to your advantage to not use. If after six months your life has not improved, you can always go back to using."

He said, "You might not have a problem with using, but it looks like your using is problematic, and needs to be addressed."

Brent said, "I lost my job and got depressed. I also broke up with my girlfriend, which didn't help the depression." The counselor told us to go to the lounge area and to talk it out. Once we got there, Brent was furious with me.

He started yelling, "This is the way I am, so deal with it."

Tim said, "Don't talk to your mother like that." I started crying. Tim tried to talk some sense into Brent, but he was not listening. We went back to the room with the counselor and psychiatrist. They asked if we had decided on a plan. We just sat there staring at them. We surely didn't have a plan. The counselor said they would release him to us if we would stay with him for the weekend. We agreed and signed the papers, releasing Brent into our care. He also told Brent that he wanted him to go to an Alcoholic Anonymous meeting sometime that day. He gave Brent a meeting schedule and asked him for his word that he would go. That was encouraging to me. I have to say that the counselor was excellent. He used several approaches with Brent to try and break through the denial of the disease. I believe that this guy was one of the angels that God sent our way during a very bad time.

We went to Brent's apartment and what we saw was very disturbing. It looked as if it had not been cleaned in quite a while. There were beer bottles all over the place. Tim and I started cleaning up. I needed to use the restroom so I went down the hall. There was blood everywhere, in the bathroom, down the hallway, and in the bedrooms. I felt like I was going to throw up. There was no way I could clean it up. Kelly, along with her mother and father showed up. Kelly still had some things to move out of the apartment.

Tim decided we needed to leave the apartment, it wasn't helping Brent emotionally to see Kelly move her things. Tim called around and got us a hotel for the rest of the weekend. The hotel we stayed at had a beautiful courtyard with waterfalls and plants. They also had a sitting area with a computer. It was very peaceful there I'm so thankful to Tim for moving us there.

The rest of the weekend, we talked with Brent a lot about what his plans were. I'm not sure if he heard anything we said, but we tried. We ate out every meal, which Brent enjoyed. I was glad to see he was eating, he looked very thin.

We also went to the movies and saw Fever Pitch with Drew Barrymore. It was a comedy, which is what we needed.

We asked Brent numerous times to please come back to Michigan with us, but he would not. It was hard saying goodbye, but we had no choice. It was an extremely emotional weekend. I prayed constantly and cried a lot. My good friend Ysabelle called and said she was praying for us.

Once we said our goodbyes, we headed for the airport. Brent was driving ahead of us. We saw him jump the cement medium, cross over in front of oncoming cars, and end up in a gas station. Tim and I sat there in disbelief. Once again, Brent was living on the edge. I really felt powerless at that moment. I'm his mother and there was nothing I could do to save him. When he was little, his problems were also little, and I could fix them. Now that he was an adult and addicted, my hands were tied. I prayed for God to save him, because I knew that I could not.

CHAPTER 22
SUMMER 2005

Brent was unemployed for the first part of the summer. He sold his custom truck and decided he wanted to go to Los Angeles and live on the beach. We tried to talk him out of it, but he went anyway. He drove for three days to get there. Once he was there, he tried to buy some drugs and had an altercation with a gang. Within 30 minutes of arriving, he turned around and headed back for Green Bay.

Once back in Green Bay, we communicated with him weekly, and finally in July, we talked him into coming to live with us in Michigan.

The first three months were wonderful. He went to work for Tim at the shop. He was eating good and seemed to be functioning. We were able to do a lot of the things that we had been longing to do with him. We camped at the state parks. We went to the Woodward Dream Cruise, which was something Brent had always wanted to do. Before, Tim and I would go and take pictures and send them to Brent. It was so awesome that this summer, he got to sit and watch the cars in person.

He was able to attend the family reunion and catch up with the relatives from his Grandpa Herb's side of the family. For three months, I felt like I could breath again. I was secure in the feeling that Brent was in a warm house and his needs were being met, but it was a false sense of security. Little did I know that the disease was lurking and ready to strike at any time.

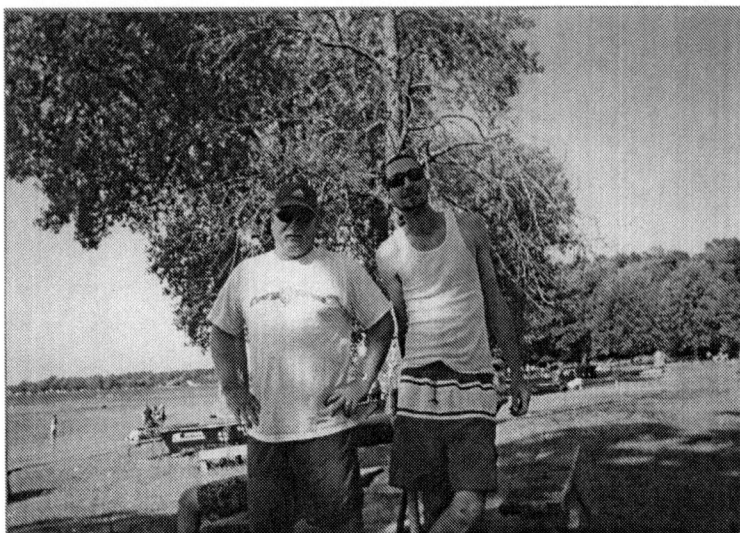

Tim and Brent at the lake

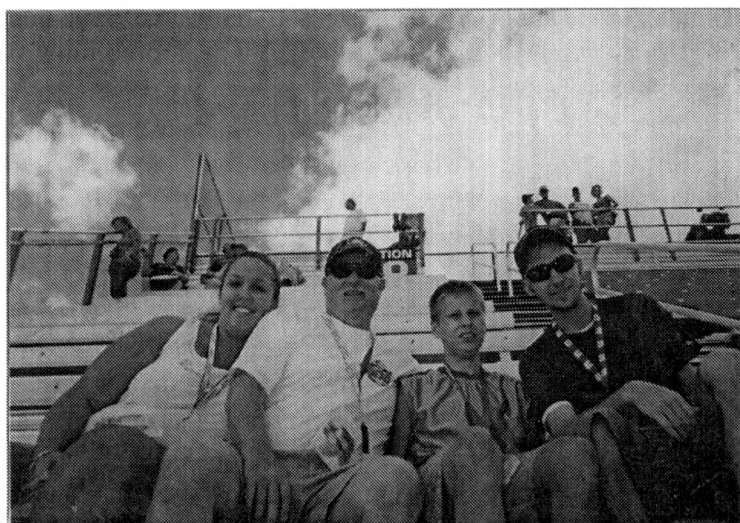

Grace, Tim, Tommy and Brent at the Nascar Race

Brent's truck

The last family photo taken with Brent October 2005

CHAPTER 23
TUESDAY DINNERS

My mom suggested we get together as a family once a week for dinner. We decided to meet on Tuesdays. One week, we would meet at my house, and the next week we would go to their house. It was a way for us all to connect as a family. My dad was the cook when I was growing up and his meals were awesome. He made many of his meals from scratch. Sunday afternoon dinners were always extra special.

We still carry on this tradition even though Brent is gone. We no longer come to my house. My dad had knee surgery a year ago and it was hard for him to get out of the house, so we started meeting at their house weekly. One week they cook, and the next week I bring take out.

Tim says he only gets a home-cooked meal twice a month when we go to my parents for dinner! Kelly also comes to dinner when she is in town!

CHAPTER 24
TRIP TO GREEN BAY

In October, Brent shaved his head. In the past when Brent was using drugs heavily, he would do that. He and Tim had words about it, and on Friday, Brent got his paycheck from Tim at lunchtime, cashed it and headed to Green Bay. The phone started ringing even before he got there with issues. He went to Kelly's apartment drunk. She called Tim crying, and asked him to call the police because Brent was trying to beat the door down.

Brent went to a friend's house for the night. I was able to talk to his friend and I asked him to tell Brent that we loved him and to come back. Brent went back over to Kelly's and the police were called again. This time, they told Brent to go back to Michigan or they were going to arrest him. He decided to head back to Michigan. He went to get on the expressway and ran off the side of the road into a deep ravine. He thought he would have to call a tow truck, but he was able to get the car out on his own. He did, however, damage the exhaust on his car while driving out.

When he got back to Michigan, we had an intervention. Tim, my parents and I sat Brent down in our living room and told him he needed help. We talked him to him about going into Detox at a local rehabilitation center in the area. He agreed to go. Tim dropped him off on Tuesday. He called Tim several times while he was in there. I came home from work on Thursday and Brent was sitting in his car in my driveway. He gave me a paper from the rehab center that said, "Go to AA meetings." He told me the center had released him. Later, I found out they didn't release him at all; he had walked.

CHAPTER 25

ACCIDENT

Tim and I decided to go up north to our cabin for Tim's birthday. We dropped Tommy off at his grandma's for the weekend and headed north. We were tired from working all day, but excited to be getting away. We had gotten about 20 miles when Tim's cell phone rang. It was one of Tim's employees calling. He was very upset and told Tim that there had been a terrible accident. He said that Brent was driving and hit someone in front of the shop. He didn't know how badly Brent was hurt, but he said it didn't look good. My heart sank. The police got on the phone and told Tim to stop driving and pull in somewhere and wait. The Jaws of Life were being called in to get Brent out of the car.

Once they could get him out, they would decide where to take him for treatment. They told us to just hold tight. The police called and said that he was alive and they would be taking him to St. Joseph Mercy Hospital in Ypsilanti. We pulled up to the hospital as the helicopter was landing. I ran over to the helicopter and was able to get close enough to see that Brent was awake. I made some phone calls to let our family know what had happened. Someone called our Pastor and he came right away. Brent had started drinking on his way to work that morning. He knew that Tim would not be there, so he would not get into trouble. He remembered getting into the car in the afternoon, but nothing after that.

The medical team was very irritated with Brent because he had been drinking. He was also not cooperating, so the staff was frustrated. When the doctor called us back, he said that other than being banged up and bruised, Brent would be OK. I thanked God for once again sparing Brent's life. Later, I found out his blood alcohol level was .09. The legal limit in Michigan is .01.

He was facing some trouble with the law due to this accident, and was also fired from his job.

CHAPTER 26
DEATH

Brent had a lot of time on his hands due to losing his job. He filled that time by using drugs night and day. I was really having a hard time with this. On the Saturday after Thanksgiving, I told Brent he had to either go into treatment for his problem or leave. He said that he liked getting high and drinking, and he was not going into treatment.

I said, "Then you have to leave."

He asked, "Now?" and I said yes. I cried as I was folding his clothes into a laundry basket for him to take with him. I asked him one more time before he left to please go into treatment.

He said, "If you take me there, I'll walk. I hugged and kissed him and told him I loved him. I cried for days after he left.

That night, he drove to Green Bay. He contacted Tim on Monday and Wednesday, and said he was applying for jobs. Tim said that he sounded good. He also contacted Kelly and she told him to call her on Friday. That was the last time anyone heard from him.

Sunday morning, it was snowing and a guy plowing the parking lot of a clinic found Brent unresponsive in his car. Brent must have not felt well and gone to the clinic to wait for it to open. An autopsy later showed that Brent died from carbon monoxide poisoning. The vents in his car were closed due to a bad repair on the vehicle. His death was ruled accidental.

Even though the police report states his death was accidental from carbon monoxide poisoning, I believe his death was the direct result of his alcohol and drug use.

If he had chosen recovery, he would have had a place to live. He would not have been sleeping in his car that cold winter's night.

The police contacted the office of the apartment building that Brent used to live at, which they got from his driver's license. They office staff gave them Kelly's forwarding address. The police went to Kelly's apartment and asked if she knew Brent Legault. She said yes and then they asked her to identify him by his driver's license. They informed her that he had passed on.

Kelly called us on Sunday afternoon, but we were at a church play. Once the play was over and we were in our car, we got her voicemail asking us to call her. She also said something about the police. I knew Brent was gone by the tone of Tim's voice when he talked to Kelly. He said, "No." I asked Tim if Brent was dead, and he started crying and said, "Yes." I started screaming at the top of my lungs. I told Tim to pull the car over, I needed to get out. He said, "No, we'll be home in ten minutes. I just kept screaming. Tim continued to cry.

I decided I needed to call someone at church to pray for us. I called one of the ladies, but she was not home. I felt really bad because I left an awful voicemail message on her phone. Then I called the Pastor's wife. She was wonderful and prayed with me. I was able to calm down until we got home. When we got home, Tim called the police department. He went down in the basement to make the call so he could have some privacy.

My brother and his wife were the first to arrive at the house. I was very touched by this. They are extremely close to their three children and when they got to my house, I asked where the kids were and Suzy said she left them in the middle of the family room hugging and crying. We all three hugged each other and cried. Then I started yelling and hitting my fists on the counter.

My brother reached over to stop me, but Suzy said, "No, Mickey, let her be." Suzy knew I needed to get my feelings out. Grace was at work and I knew someone needed to go get her. My brother volunteered. We contacted her at work and told her that Mickey would be picking her up. Grace later told me she thought something bad had happened to either me or Brent.

Some of the ladies that she works with waited with her in the lobby until Mickey got there. They are the sweetest group of ladies. I can never repay them for their kindness to Grace.

Once Grace got in the car, Mickey told her Brent was gone. She said she cried for a while and then when Mickey thought she was ready, they started to drive to our house.

I was very touched by Mickey's selfless act. He didn't even hesitate when we asked someone to go get her. I'm forever indebted to him for this.

My parents arrived at the house next, then my sister. Other people came during the evening. I went from yelling to crying to being OK. It was awful. Around 9:00 pm everyone left. Tim went to bed, which left Grace and I alone in our grief. We took turns crying all night long. I would cry and she would hold me, then she would cry and I would hold her. It was just awful.

The next morning, Tim went to work to get the shop opened up.

I knew I needed to get some sleeping pills for Grace and I. I called my dad to see if he would come over and stay with Tommy while Grace and I went to the ER.

Thankfully, Tim came home and drove us to the ER. They were really wonderful there. The doctor gave us both scripts with enough sleeping pills to get through the week.

Once we got home, my family came over. I remember the house phone and everyone's cell phones ringing constantly.

Janet, one of the ladies I work with, brought over a big pot of homemade chicken noodle soup. I couldn't eat it, but my family did and they said it was wonderful. Her kind gesture of love touched my heart deeply.

One of my coworkers, Chris, and her sister, Patty, came over with bags and bags of groceries. Chris took up a collection at work and then went to the store for us. Many other collections were taken up and we were able to make a sizeable donation in Brent's name to a local drug and alcohol rehabilitation facility. I have no words to express how deeply everyone's kindness has touched me.

CHAPTER 27
FUNERAL

We went to the funeral home to make arrangements on Monday.

It was so very hard. Grace and I had not slept at all on Sunday night, and Tim only slept two hours. It was very cold that day and there was snow on the ground.

My parents came to pick us up in their van. For some reason, the van doors would not close.

I remember sitting in the van with both sliding doors open and freezing. I was thinking, "I should not be sitting here. I should be anywhere but here. I'm cold, tired and sick with grief."

My dad finally got the doors to close and we headed to the funeral home.

The director had us go downstairs for the meeting. It was a long, dark hallway. It all seemed like a dream. I kept thinking, "What am I doing here? I'm not supposed to be at a funeral home making funeral plans for my son. He should be alive and vibrant." After all, he was only 23 years old. We all sat in a room with a long boardroom table. I remember the chairs being comfy. Thankfully, my Pastor, who had been out of town, was able to make the meeting. He drove all night to get there. He is an awesome man of God. We are so very blessed to have him in our lives.

The director said, "We will start by deciding when you

would like the funeral to take place."

I replied, "As soon as possible." I just wanted to get it over with. He said that the obituary needed to be in the paper for a day and it was too late to go into Monday's paper.

Then he said, "Usually, you have one day for the viewing with the funeral the following day." I was thinking that it was too long, I didn't know if I would hold up. My mother agreed with the director so I said OK. The viewing would be on Wednesday and the funeral on Thursday.

I was thinking, "What am I going to do all day Tuesday?" It seemed like the day would be endless and I wouldn't be able to hold up.

The director was called out of the meeting for a phone call. When he came back, he said he was on the phone with the Green Bay funeral home and they said that due to the condition of the body, we wouldn't be able to have an open casket. I just lost it, I cried and said no. I would never again be able to look at my son. I was crushed. The director said that it was very costly to fly the body to Michigan and we might want to think about cremation. I asked the pastor if there was anything in the bible that said you should not cremate and he said no. Kelly said that she and Brent had discussed what they wanted to do when they died, and Brent said he wanted to be cremated.

Tim got very upset, and said, "Wait a minute, I want to think about." I asked him if he had a problem with cremation and he said no, but he wanted to make sure it was what we all agreed on. We all talked about it for a few minutes and then agreed that it would be best to cremate.

The ashes did not arrive in time for the funeral. Due to his body being in another state, there was a lot of red tape to work through. For some reason, the Green Bay funeral home had his name listed as Brent Allan. When they sent the paperwork to the Michigan director, he caught the mix up. The paperwork had to be corrected on our end and sent back to Green Bay before the cremation could take place.

Grace had taken a medical class through school, which had required her to visit the morgue. She was devastated to think her brother was in the morgue for days on end. I kept reassuring her it was just his body and that he was actually in heaven. Even though I stayed strong for Grace, it also tore at my heart.

After the plans were made, my parents dropped me off at home. My family then went to the flower shop to order flowers for the funeral. I took some sleeping pills and went to bed. Rhonda came into my bedroom and stood next to my bed. She listened to me cry about how unfair it was that Brent was gone. She kept telling me she knew it was unfair and that she was sorry. Grace and Kelly came up to my room after they got back from ordering the flowers and sat on the end of my bed. I just kept crying while they tried to console me. I believe that was the darkest moment of my life. I cannot tell you what I would have done if they had not been there with me. I know it had to be difficult for them to listen to me sob as my heart was breaking. I will never forget their kindness and compassion. Not very many people can withstand the emotional toll it takes to be with someone while they are suffering like that. That night, they were my angels.

There were over 200 people that came to the funeral home for the viewing. Many of the people were coworkers of mine. There was a long line of people waiting to talk to me and give me hugs. It was heartwarming that so many people reached out to us.

Our church would not be able to accommodate the funeral service so we used the Church of God we used to attend. They had built a new sanctuary that was very beautiful.

We asked two members of the church to sing, which

was very nice. Brent's Grandma Patty read a letter I had written to Brent. Tommy also read a letter he had written to Brent. They were both so brave. When the Pastor asked us to stand for the reading of the Gospel, I thought I was going to pass out. I kept thinking to myself, "Hang in there; if you pass out; it will just take longer." Thankfully, I made it through the reading and was able to sit down. The Pastor preached a heartfelt message that reached many of the people that were there.

After the funeral, the ladies from our church and the Church of God served a very nice dinner. I was feeling a little better at that point and was able to eat some chicken. After dinner, we went back to the sanctuary to decide what to do with the flowers and plants. What we didn't take would be given to the area nursing homes. I took a peace lily and when I got home, I placed it next to the piano that Brent used to play.

On New Year's Day, we put Brent's remains to rest. He is in a niche at a cemetery in Ypsilanti.

My Grandma Lucille is buried there as well. My parents, along with my Uncle Alton and Aunt Joanne have plots there. I have a very hard time going to the cemetery. When I go there, I can no longer deny that he's gone. It's not a bad dream that I can wake up from. It usually takes me days to stop crying.

CHAPTER 28
BARB'S WORKPLACE

Within one year, five employees where I work lost their children.

Bill was the first; he lost his daughter in May 2005. In December, I lost Brent. New Year's Eve, Carl lost his son. Valentine's Day Karen lost her son, and on Mother's Day, Shelia lost her daughter.

Statistically, this is very unusual.

We all have stuck together through this. We check on each other, especially at holidays and heavenly dates. We have shed many tears together.

Carl and Karen have since retired, but they are often in my thoughts and prayers.

Carl and his wife are raising their daughter's children. The children are blessed to have such caring grandparents.

Brent did not have any children. My dreams of being a grandmother to his children are gone.

I will never get to see who they would look like. I won't get to see them start kindergarten or play softball. I won't get to take them to church or sit in the audience of a school play.

Not only did Brent die that day, but all my dreams of what our life would be like together also died. Sometimes, life can be very cruel.

CHAPTER 29
COMMUNICATION

Soon after Brent's death, we would feel and see him at our home.

We would hear him running up and down the stairs. It woke Tommy up several times and each time, he yelled, "Who is running up and down the stairs waking me up?"

Tim yelled back, "It's Brent."

Tommy was playing with his toys on the floor and one of his trucks with missiles shot one off. He said it scared him and he told Brent to stop, he was scaring him.

Tim sees Brent a lot. He hear him walking across the kitchen floor. One winter night, he saw Brent walking through the house with no shoes or socks on. Tim asked Brent if he had shoes and socks on, and Brent nodded that he didn't and went downstairs.

Brent and Tim used to watch a high-end car auction on TV together. Now when Tim watches it, Brent shows up. He sits in the chair next to the couch.

A few weeks after his death, I couldn't sleep so I went into the family room and lay down on the couch. Where I was laying was the last place Brent had sat. I said to myself, "This might not be a good idea," but I did it anyway. About an hour after I fell asleep, I was awakened by someone giving me a hug. I jumped up. I thought it was Tim, but no one was around. I cried and cried after I got that hug from Brent, it meant so much to me.

One night, I dreamt that I was at Tim's sister's house. It wasn't the house she's in now.

They were having a birthday party for someone and all of my family was there, along with Tim's family. Brent came to the party. He looked really good. He was wearing a white t-shirt and jeans. He came over to me and started hugging me. I yelled for everyone to come over and they did, and we all had a group hug. I woke up in tears. It was awesome that he came and hugged everyone. It is comforting when he comes to me. He is smiling and looks healthy.

About a year after Brent's death, I was typing on my computer at work. I was trying to send out a text page to someone, and the keys twice spelled out Brent. I looked down at the keyboard to see if I had my fingers in the wrong position, but they weren't. Brent came to me that day because he knew I was under a lot of stress. My mother was not doing well. She had two leaking heart valves that required open-heart surgery. She has since recovered from that surgery, and is doing very well.

Brent may be gone from this world as we know it, but spiritually, he stays in touch.

I believe it is God's way of softening the loss for us.

CHAPTER 30
TOMMY'S MEMORIES

B rent and Tommy were best buddies. They would wrestle each other constantly.

Tim was always yelling at them to stop before something got broke.

When we were building the house we live in today, we rented an apartment for nine months. We lived there during the winter months. Brent came for Christmas that year and showed Tommy how to ride his sled down the stairs at the apartment building.

We lived on the third floor, so it was quite a ride! One night, when Tim came home from work, he noticed a lot of scratches on the walls and he wondered if someone had damaged the walls moving in. Then he saw Tommy and his friend coming down the stairs on the sled. Tim said, "What are you doing?"

Tommy said, "Brent showed us how to do this!"

At the end of each flight of stairs was a huge plate glass window, which they could easily have gone flying out of! Brent told them it was more fun to do it inside because it wasn't so cold!

Tommy had a dirt bike. He would ride it up and down the driveway and around the house.

There was a little hill that he liked to jump over by the side of the house. Brent decided he wanted to ride the bike.

He started at the end of the street and hit it full throttle up the hill. He went flying in the air. Tommy said he went higher than the motor home. He crashed, flipped and landed just short of the fence in the backyard. Tommy thought Brent was dead, but he only hurt his wrist. That's how Brent lived his life; 100 mph on the edge all the time.

Grace and Tim love Nascar racing. Grace's favorite driver is Jeff Gordon. Tim likes most drivers except Jeff Gordon and Jimmy Johnson! They have a running feud every year over who is the better driver. We go to MIS Speedway in the Irish Hills for two races every year. We take our motor home and stay on the track campgrounds for the weekend. One year, Tommy was riding Brent around the campground on the handlebars of his bike. Tommy said they were checking out hot girls!

Brent was not a Nascar fan, but he enjoyed all the action at the racetrack.

Jeremy Mayfield won the race. Brent was clapping and high-fiving everyone.

Grace hit him and said, "You are such a rookie, Jeremy is a nobody." She was mad that her guy didn't win. Brent was having a blast!

CHAPTER 31
FUNNY MEMORIES

Brent had a great sense of humor. He loved to laugh and joke around. Tim loved playing practical jokes on him. One time, Brent was at home by himself watching a horror movie. He was downstairs and had all the lights on in the basement. He also had a blanket over his head, only peaking out of one side to see the TV. Tim came home and decided to try and scare Brent. He tapped on the basement window then hid by the bushes. Brent looked out the window, but didn't see anyone so he went back to watching his show. Tim tapped on the window again and Brent ran outside to try and catch whoever was doing it. Later, Tim strolled into the house acting like he didn't know what was going on. When Brent told him that someone was tapping on the window, Tim confessed and said it was him. Brent said he would get Tim back for that one.

Another time, Brent was coming up the basement stairs and Tim grabbed the doorknob and stood around the corner. Brent kept trying to get the door open, but he thought it was stuck. Tim almost gave the joke away by laughing. When Tim finally let go of the door, and Brent came out, he laughed and said he figured it was Tim blocking the door.

One of the funniest jokes Tim played on Brent was when he put voicemail on our phone line.

Tim didn't tell Brent that he had done this. When there

was a message, the phone would beep when you picked it up. Brent thought for sure the phone was bugged. This went on for a few weeks. Finally, Brent was at his grandma Mary Lou's house and he went to use the phone, and it was beeping. He asked his grandma what the beeping noise was, and she said it meant she had a voicemail message. When Brent told Tim he knew the phone wasn't bugged, we all had a good laugh.

Brent was also very talented. He was a musician and artist. He played the piano beautifully.

He also liked to draw and paint. One year for Christmas, he drew me a picture of a rose. I kept it; it's very beautiful.

Another Christmas, he painted a picture of a single red rose on a canvas. He also painted one for both of his grandmas. We all have them on display in our homes today.

CHAPTER 32
TAPE / CD

B rent loved to play our piano. He would also play the harmonica and sing.

He bought a little hand-held tape recorder and he would tape himself singing and playing.

When he passed away, the police confiscated the tape and listened to it. They wanted to make sure there wasn't a suicide note on it. When Kelly got the tape back, the ribbon was broken. She put the tape away, but intended some day to have it fixed and the contents of it put on a CD. I asked Kelly a few times if she had taken the tape to get it fixed, but she said she couldn't bring herself to do it. Kelly emailed me in January 2007 to say she would be coming to Michigan for the weekend. I asked her if she would please bring the tape with her, and she did.

I put the tape in a sandwich bag and put it in my purse. I knew it was in there all week, but I couldn't look at it.

I have so very few personal items of Brent's and I knew this one was a real treasure.

I ended up taking it to a video business that could fix the tape and transfer it to a CD.

I felt bad for the guy that helped me because I was crying. I told the guy that my son had passed away and the tape was of him singing and playing the piano. The guy felt really bad for me. I felt really bad for him! He said they would take care of it and to come back in one week.

I went to the video store on Friday after work. I got the tape back along with the CD.

I put the CD in my car stereo, but it wouldn't work. I said to Brent, "Are you messing with me?" I called the guy at the video store and he said sometimes CDs are not compatible with certain stereos. He told me to try it in another CD player. I took it home and put it in a CD player I had there. Sure enough, it worked. I listened to the entire CD. It was 50 minutes long. It was very hard to hear his voice again. I cried while I listened to it. I also cried myself to sleep that night.

I made copies of the CD and gave them to my mom and Tim. I also sent one to Kelly.

Little did I know when Brent was taping himself that someday, the tape would mean so much to me.

CHAPTER 33
MEMORIAL RIDE

Tim and I have a 2005 Harley Davidson Road King. Tim put a custom paint job on it and turned the bike into a memorial for Brent. Tim got the idea from our piano at home. He took a picture of the piano with the painting of the red rose on it and gave it to a friend of his that does custom work. She digitally enhanced the photo and painted the keys of our keyboard on the bike tank. She also painted a red rose laying across the keys. We also have musical notes going down the side of the bike with Brent's name and the year he passed away. When we are out riding, people call Tim the piano man. It means a lot to us when people ask how we came up with the piano theme, and we are able to tell them about Brent. It's one way that we can keep his memory alive. Tim has entered the bike in a few shows and has won awards with it.

Soon after Brent's death, we decided to have a memorial motorcycle ride in Brent's memory. His 24th birthday would have been Saturday, August 5th. We decided that would be a good day for the ride.

We started planning it in February. I booked the UAW hall from my work. We made up fliers and put them at Harley dealerships. I listed the ride on every website I could find. I also posted fliers at work.

The ride went very smoothly. We prayed that everyone

would be safe and have a good time.

We had 50 bikes and 100 people. My parents and their special friend, Linda, came to help with registration and the dinner after the ride. My very good friends, Yvonne and John, also helped with the registration. My brother and sister-in-law helped set up the food. One of Tim's employees, Mike, brought the pork we had ordered. Many of my family came later for the dinner. Kelly came in from Green Bay. Some of the employees at Grace's work took up a collection, and one of the ladies dropped it off during registration. We were very touched by this caring gesture.

It turned out to be a warm and sunny day. I felt Brent's presence with us. His love shined down on us. There were a few tears, but all in all, it was the first time since I lost him that I felt at peace.

We plan on having the ride annually. It will be the first Saturday of August.

We donated all the proceeds to a local alcohol and drug rehabilitation center in our area.

I figure I might not have been able to help Brent while he was alive, but if I can help someone else's child then Brent's death will not have been in vain. I don't want any parent to have to face the devastating loss that we have had to endure.

Tim and Barb's Harley painted in memory of Brent

Memorial Ride 2006

CHAPTER 34
THREE SPECIAL WOMEN

I would like to acknowledge three very special women in my life.

The first is my friend Rhonda. I have known her for many years.

Our children have grown up together. We have shared the joys of our life, as well as the heartaches. Rhonda has been a huge help throughout this lonely path of grief that I have found myself on. She understands because she suffered the loss of her dear husband George. When we talk to each other, we know exactly where the other one is coming from. She knows the pain and depression that I'm going through first-hand. I can talk to her about anything. Rhonda is a very kind and loving person. I'm very blessed to have her as a friend.

Shelia is my next special friend. I have worked with her for many years. We became close friends after her daughter passed away. I'm so sorry that the death of our children has been our bond, but I'm so very thankful to have her in my life.

We check on each other often. All she has to do is take one look at me to know how I'm feeling. She is a little harder to read. I have to talk to her for a minute or two to see if she is OK.

When I need someone to talk to, she's right there. We both have good days and bad days. We are not sure what our futures will hold, but I do know that I can count on her to be there for me. She also knows that I will be right there by her side every step of the way.

Last but certainly not least is Betty. She is Tim's maternal aunt who lives in Pahrump, Nevada. We have corresponded for many years through letters and emails. When Brent passed away, she couldn't be with me, but she called daily. Every week for one solid year, she sent us a card. She would tell us what was going on in her life and that she was praying for us. I know it's been her many prayers that have held us together. It is rare to find such a loving and caring person. She is truly an example of God's love in action.

CHAPTER 35
ENDING

In closing, I would like to say that I loved Brent more than I could ever express in words. He was such a bright spot in my life. As I look back on his childhood, my heart smiles with so many warm memories of him. He was funny and smart. We had so much fun together as a family. He is so very missed. There is not a day that goes by that my heart doesn't break when I think of him. I don't know what my future holds, but I can tell you that there is a deep, deep hole in my heart that will never be filled. A part of me died that Saturday night with Brent. Someone told me not to climb into the grave with him and I try very hard not to. I try to stay busy and do things that will keep his memory alive. Writing this book has been bittersweet. It has been wonderful reliving the good memories, but completely torturous reliving the bad ones.

Brent, I wrote this book for you, because I'm so very proud of you. You had a disease that was more powerful than you and I. I did everything in my power to help you, but it wasn't enough.

I try not to beat myself up for that, I did what I could. I'm so very thankful that your pain and torment is over. You're resting in God's hands now, and someday I will see you again when I get to Gloryland!

God bless everyone reading this book. I pray that if you have a loved one affected by the disease, that you will seek help for yourself. You do not have to fight this fight alone.

CHAPTER 36
SPECIAL THANKS

I would like to give special thanks to my dear husband, Tim.

He is truly my knight in shining armor. I'm so thankful God put us together.

I would like to give a very special thanks to my dear, sweet daughter Grace. Her strength and courage amazes me. She stepped up to the plate during a very difficult time, and I will be forever grateful to her for that. She is my shining star!

A special thanks goes to my stepson, Tommy. He and Brent were best buddies. The love that Tommy showed Brent was heartwarming. They were not only brothers, but also best friends.

I would like to thank my parents, Herb and Mary Lou. They have always been there for me and my family no matter what. Their guidance and strength have made me the person I am today. Their love for my son leaves me speechless. I'm so very blessed to have them as parents.

Thank you to my sister, Lynn. She was my rock when we were growing up, and she still is today. I can count on her to be there at a moment's notice. She is not only my sister, but also my friend.

To my brother Mickey, his wife, Suzy, and their three children. I thank them for everything. Their kindness and support are very precious to me.

I would like to thank my Uncle Alton and Aunt Joanne. We are so very blessed to have this special couple in our lives. They have been there for us through thick and thin. I will be forever grateful to them for their love and support.

A special thanks goes out to my mom's friends, Linda and Maggie. I thank them from the bottom of my heart for being there for my mother when I was so consumed with grief.

They are both very special angels that God placed in our family many years ago.

I would like to thank my father-in-law, Glen, and mother-in-law, Reba, for raising such an awesome son. May God bless you both mightily.

Thank you to my brother-in-law, Jeff, and sister-in-law, Kim, for being with Tim in his darkest hours before I was in his life. We all need to have someone push us back into the land of the living and you both did that for him.

I would like to thank everyone I work with for their thoughts and prayers. Their concern for me and my family has been heartwarming. I'm blessed to have so many wonderful people in my life.

I would like to thank my wonderful boss, Kevin. He is such a caring and compassionate man. He greets me with a bright smile every morning! He is by far the best boss I ever had. I appreciate his kindness; it warms my heart.

I would like to give special thanks to my dear friend and coworker, Pat. Her office is always open if I need a hug or a shoulder to cry on. She will never know how many times she helped me get through a rough day. I thank her also for sharing her beautiful grandchildren with me. Someday, if I'm blessed to be a grandmother, I want to be just like her. Her family is very blessed to have her and so am I.

I also would like to thank my coworker, Dana. She was

the second person to read the rough draft of this book and she gave me valuable insight on how to improve it. I thank her for taking the time.

I would also like to thank my coworker, Melinda. Her spiritual guidance has been priceless. The books and other materials she passes on to me have strengthened my walk with God. She is an awesome prayer warrior.

I would like to thank my coworkers, Janet and La-Wanna. Many times I have called Janet in despair and asked her to pray so I could make it through the workday. She immediately finds her prayer partner, LaWanna, and they start praying. I know their prayers reach heaven because I usually feel better right away. Their kindness and concern touches my heart deeply.

I would like to thank my good friend and coworker, Yvonne. She has such a zest for life. She is by far the most giving person I have ever met. She helps so many causes and she is truly a blessing to me and my family. I thank both her and her sweetie, John, for all the help they gave us at the memorial ride.

I would also like to thank my coworker and friend, Ron. He makes me laugh almost daily, which is something everyone needs to do!

A special thanks to Vickie for being obedient and bringing her family to church. Every time I see them in the second pew my heart smiles.

Thank you Glen for all the inspirational CDs that you send my way, it has truly strengthened my walk with God. You told me that I have a new ministry now, one in which I will help other grieving parents. I didn't want to hear it at the time, but it is true. I am going to work very hard to make this ministry what God would have it be.

I would like to give a special thanks to the Prayer Circle at work. The circle is made up of forty-one mighty prayer warriors. Our Prayer Partner, Ernestine, started the circle many years ago. When she retired she asked me to oversee it. One of her special sayings was "Don't block your blessings." I reflect on this a lot and remember how true it is. Complaining will get you nowhere. Thank you, Ernestine, for the awesome legacy that you left. Thank you to the Prayer Circle for your dedication.

God bless you all!

I would like to thank my Pastor, his wife and our church members. God blessed us mightily when he led us there. They are a very special group of people.

A special thanks to Lori my photographer. You came to my home a few months before Brent passed and took incredible pictures of my family. The pictures are priceless treasures that will be here long after I am gone. God has blessed you with an awesome talent and I am very thankful that you took the time to be with my family.

I would like to thank Angel Editing for their hard work editing the book. I would not have been able to complete this project without their assistance.

Most of all, I would like to thank Our Almighty God. He comforted me in my darkest hour and carried me when I could not walk. I will praise Him all the days of my life.

Printed in the United States
200514BV00002B/169-219/A